03 YELLOW • **BOOK 2** /th/ng/

Minneapolis,

Teaching Tips

This book focuses on the phonemes **/th/ng/**.

Getting Started
- Review the focus phonemes of the book with readers.
- Model the sounds and have readers practice themselves.

Using the Book
- Ask readers to read the words on the pages with the colorful borders, using the focus sounds as their guide.
- Turn the page and check the illustration next to the word to confirm accuracy.
- As you read new words, review the word bank on the left-hand pages of the book.

Reviewing
- Encourage readers to independently reread all of the words on pages 22–23.
- Have them complete the activity on page 24 for continued practice with the focus phonemes.
- Extend the learning by asking readers if they know any other words containing the focus phonemes.

© 2025 Booklife Publishing
This edition is published by arrangement with Booklife Publishing.

North American adaptations © 2025 Bearport Publishing Company. All rights reserved. No part of this publication may be reproduced in whole or in part, stored in any retrieval system, or transmitted in any form or by any means, electronic, mechanical, photocopying, recording, or otherwise, without written permission from the publisher. Bearport Publishing is a division of Chrysalis Education Group.

For more information, write to Bearport Publishing, 5357 Penn Avenue South, Minneapolis, MN 55419.

moth

moth

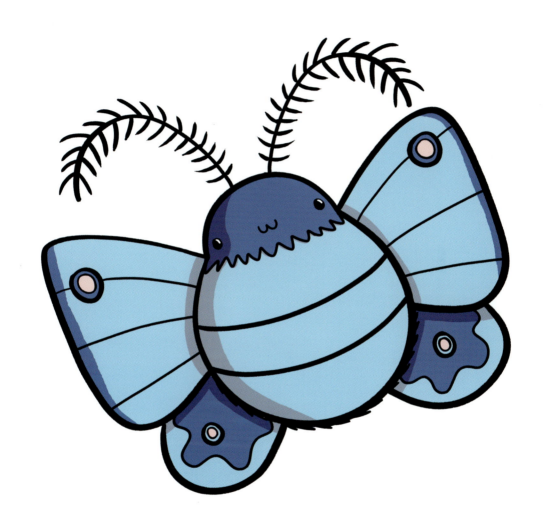

moth

math

math

math

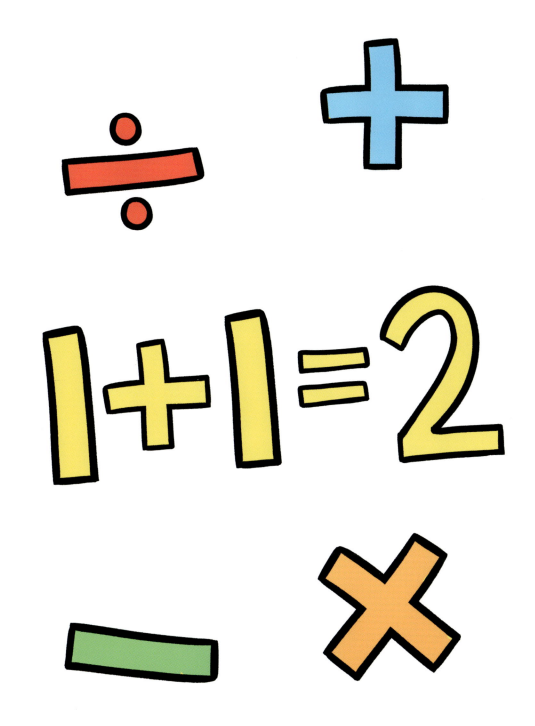

moth

math

fang

fang

fang

moth

math

fang

thin

thin

thin

moth

math

fang

thin

thick

thick

thick

moth

 math

fang

thin

thick

23

Say the sound and trace the letters with your finger.